ARCTIC TUNDRA

written by **CLAUDIA OVIEDO**

ISBN-13: 978-0-328-94185-8
ISBN-10:   0-328-94185-9
4 19

Treeless land stretches out. It seems to touch the edge of the sky. This natural wonder is the tundra. It is the coldest place on Earth to live.

There are two types of tundra. Alpine tundra is high in the mountains. Arctic tundra is near the North Pole.

Alpine tundra

Arctic tundra

THE WORLD'S ARCTIC TUNDRA

CANADA

Alaska

UNITED
STATES

N
W E
S

Areas of Arctic Tundra

Arctic tundra covers one tenth of Earth's surface.
Many northern countries have tundra. Canada and
the United States have tundra.

Many plants and animals live in the Arctic tundra. In Alaska, brown bears live in the tundra. The Alaskan tundra is also home to polar bears.

brown bears

polar bears

WILDLIFE REFUGES IN ALASKA

CANADA

Alaska

N
W ⬢ E
S

Wildlife Refuge

Many areas of land in Alaska are part of wildlife refuges. A refuge protects the plants and animals that live there.

Seasons in the ARCTIC TUNDRA

Arctic tundra winters are cold. They last from September to April. During these months, there is little or no sunlight. The ground stays frozen.

During winter, the sun never rises very high in the sky over the Arctic tundra.

Arctic tundra summers last from May to August. The sun stays in the sky all day and all night.

In summer, the sun shines even at midnight in the Arctic tundra.

The summer sun warms the Arctic tundra soil. The top few inches of soil thaw. The thawed soil is called the active layer. The frozen soil underneath the active layer is called permafrost. Permafrost never thaws.

ARCTIC TUNDRA SOIL

Active Layer

Permafrost

In summer, the ice in the active layer becomes water. In some places, the water forms pools. Some of the bigger pools are lakes.

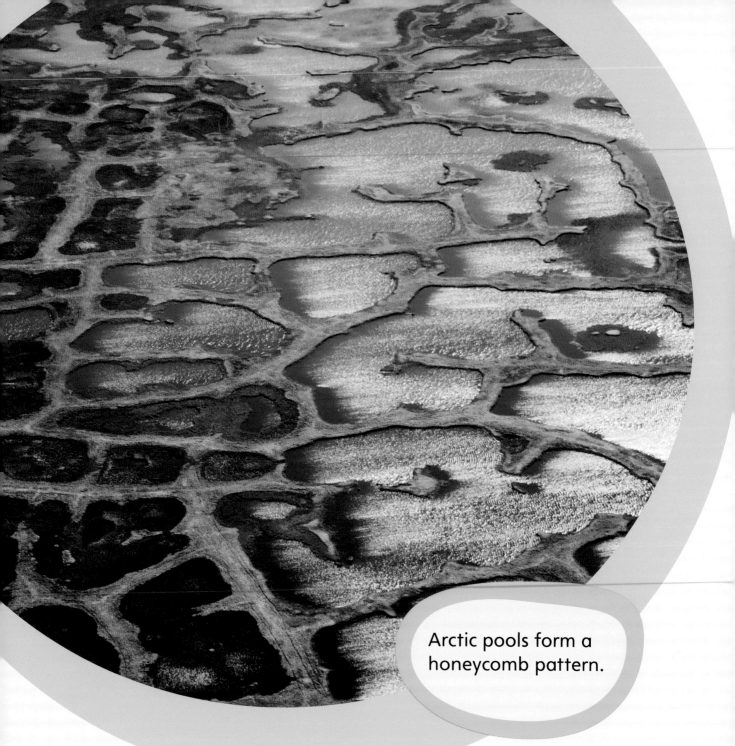

Arctic pools form a honeycomb pattern.

In some places, the Arctic soil gets very dry. Then it cracks. Water flows down the cracks. In winter, the water in the cracks freezes. The ice in the cracks forms wedges. Pools form between wedges.

Plants and Animals
in the ARCTIC TUNDRA

The top layer of Artic tundra soil is shallow. It is not deep enough for tree roots. Plants that grow here are not very tall. They include shrubs, grasses, mosses, and lichens.

grasses

shrubs

lichens

mosses

Lemmings eat plants and lichens. They also eat roots, berries, and seeds.

Plants in the Arctic tundra are food for many animals. Insects and small animals, including lemmings and Arctic squirrels, eat them. Birds also eat the plants.

14

caribou

musk ox

Arctic tundra plants are also food for large animals. Sheep and caribou nibble on grasses and moss. Musk oxen eat them too.

In the winter, the Arctic fox has white fur. The camouflage makes the fox hard to see on the snow and ice. In the summer, the fox's fur is brown.

Many plant eaters, such as lemmings and Arctic hares, are prey. Larger animals hunt them. These larger animals include Arctic foxes and brown bears.

ARCTIC TUNDRA FOOD CHAIN

brown bear

Arctic hare

plants

A food chain shows how food energy passes from one living thing to another. In the Arctic tundra, the brown bear is at the top of the food chain. It gets energy from eating prey such as the Arctic hare. The hare gets energy from eating plants.

17

large animal

small animal

plants and berries

fish

Brown bears eat almost anything. They eat roots and berries. They eat worms and insects. They eat fish, small animals, and even caribou.

Alaskan brown bears catch salmon in rivers.

In summer, brown bears travel. They wander far looking for food. They must fatten up for winter.

Animals of the Coastal ARCTIC TUNDRA

On the coast, small fish are food for other animals. Birds catch them from above. Ringed seals catch them under the ice.

Ringed seal pups are food for other animals too. Arctic foxes and polar bears hunt them on land. Whales hunt them in the water.

Ringed seals are the smallest kind of seal.

COASTAL ARCTIC FOOD WEB

Along the Arctic coast, polar bears are the top hunters in the food web. A food web, like a food chain, shows how energy passes from plants to animals to other animals. This food web shows that polar bears eat both seals and birds. Seals and birds, in turn, eat fish and smaller ocean animals, including shrimp.

ringed seal

shrimp

polar bear

Arctic birds

People in the ARCTIC TUNDRA

People also live on the tundra. One group of people is the Iñupiat. Many of them live in Kaktovik. About 300 people live in this town. Kaktovik is on an island in northern Alaska.

The Iñupiat dry salmon by hanging it from wood poles.

The Iñupiat eat some plants and berries. They eat meat from birds, seals, and other animals. They also eat fish and other ocean animals.

The Iñupiat hunt whales for food. Polar bears feed
on the leftover whale bones.

Challenges in the ARCTIC TUNDRA

Long ago, people hunted harbor seals. They ate the meat. They made clothing out of seal skins.

Today, many people still hunt in the Arctic tundra. They hunt harbor seals for their skins. Some people think that there are too few harbor seals left.

About 100 years ago, Alaska had no musk oxen.
One reason the oxen disappeared was hunting.
People wanted the animals' thick, warm fur.

Some people thought musk oxen were important. In 1930, people captured 34 musk oxen in Greenland. They moved them to Alaska. These animals formed a new herd. Now, thousands of musk oxen live in Alaska.

A musk ox's coat has two layers. The outer layer is long and rough. The inner layer is shorter and very soft.

Winters in the Arctic tundra are becoming shorter. Summers are becoming longer. Some animals need the cold and ice. It is harder for them to find food during the longer summers.

Arctic foxes live in the Arctic tundra. They face new competition for food. As summers get longer, red foxes from the south are moving into the tundra.

Helping the ARCTIC TUNDRA

Many groups work to help the Arctic tundra. The government is helping. Scientists and native peoples are also helping. Other people who care about Earth are helping too.

Scientists are trying to help the Arctic fox. The scientists place radios on some of the foxes. This helps the scientists learn about the foxes' behavior.

The plants and animals of the Arctic tundra are connected. Each plant and animal plays an important role. Plants and animals depend on each other. That is how nature works.